This book is a gift from:

_____

To: _____
The newest University of North Carolina Tar Heel fan!

Rameses' Newest Carolina Football Fan Pledge:

I pledge allegiance to the Tar Heels of the University of North Carolina. I promise to cheer for the Tar Heels whether winning or losing, through thick and thin, for good plays and bad, in sadness and in joy, and to cherish and continually give my deepest devotion, forsaking all other teams, as long as I shall cheer for football.

Go Tar Heels, Go!

What's it Called?™

Written by John Beausang   Illustrated by Mia Bosna

RivalRompers, Inc.™
Creating the next generation of fans

Hey Rameses!
What's it Called?™

Written by John Beausang
Illustrated by Mia Bosna

RivalRompers™ is a trademark of RivalRompers, Inc.
PO BOX 744 • Wrightsville Beach, NC 28408
Library of Congress Control Number: 978-0-9833454-4-2

All rights reserved including the right of reproduction in whole or part in any form.
RivalRompers™ is a trademark of RivalRompers., Inc.
Copyright ©2011 RivalRompers, Inc.

The University of North Carolina®, UNC®, and Tar Heels® are registered trademarks of the University of North Carolina, Chapel Hill, NC. North Carolina™, Carolina™, Tar Heel™, Heels™, North Carolina Tar Heels™, Carolina Tar Heels™, Kenan Memorial Stadium™, and The Bell Tower™ are trademarks of the University of North Carolina, Chapel Hill, NC.

Hi, I'm Rameses.

And I love the Tar Heels!

Are you ready to play?

What's it called?

Carolina!

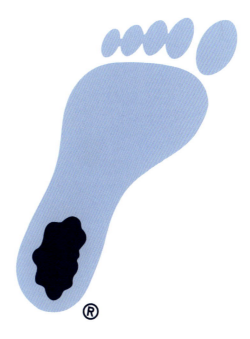

What's it called?

Tar Heel!

What's it called?

The Bell Tower!

What's it called?

The Kenan Memorial Stadium

Kenan Stadium!

What are they called?

Tar Heels!

What's it called?

Football!

What's it called when the other team has the football?

Go Defense!

What's it called when we stop the player with the ball?

Tackle!

What's it called when a player drops the football?

What's it called when the Tar Heels have the football?

What's he called?

Referee!

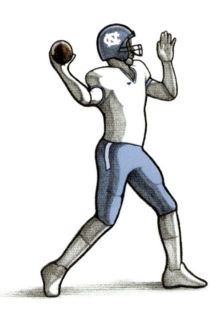

What's it called when the quarterback throws the ball?

Pass!

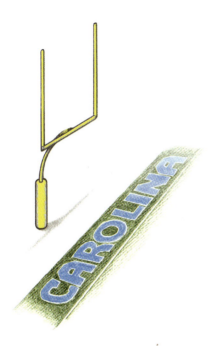

What's it called when the Tar Heels kick the football through the goal posts?

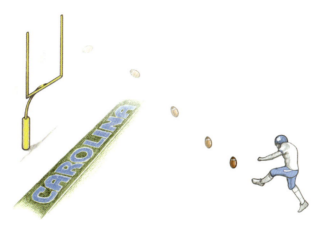

What's it called when the Tar Heels get the football into the end zone?

Touchdown!

What do we sing?

I'm a Tar Heel Born

I'm a Tar Heel born
I'm a Tar Heel bred
And when I die
I'm a Tar Heel dead.
So it's Rah, Rah, Car'lina-lina
Rah, Rah, Car'lina-lina
Rah, Rah, Car'lina
Rah! Rah! Rah!

Hark the Sound

Hark the sound of Tar Heel voices
Ringing clear and true.
Singing Carolina's praises.
Shouting N-C-U.
Hail to the brightest star of all
Clear its radiance shine
Carolina priceless gem.
Receive all praises thine.